Hertfordshire

CHO

Please renew/return this item by the last date shown.

So that your telephone call is charged at local rate,
please call the numbers as set out below:

	From Area codes 01923 or 020:	From the rest of Herts:
Renewals:	01923 471373	01438 737373
Enquiries:	01923 471333	01438 737333
Textphone:	01923 471599	01438 737599

L32   www.hertsdirect.org/librarycatalogue

D1351222

H45 839 610 4

explaining...

BLINDNESS

W

FRANKLIN WATTS
LONDON•SYDNEY

First published in 2009 by
Franklin Watts
338 Euston Road
London NW1 3BH

Franklin Watts Australia
Level 17/207 Kent Street
Sydney NSW 2000

© 2009 Franklin Watts

ISBN 978 0 7496 8255 2

Dewey classification number: 362.1'97712

All rights reserved. No part of this publication may
be reproduced, stored in a retrieval system, or
transmitted in any form or by any means,
electronic, mechanical, photocopying, recording or
otherwise, without the prior written permission of
the copyright owner.

A CIP catalogue record for this publication is
available from the British Library.

Planning and production by Discovery Books Limited
Managing Editor: Laura Durman
Editor: Gianna Williams
Designer: Keith Williams
Picture research: Rachel Tisdale
Consultants: Suzy McDonald and Stevie Johnson

Printed in China

Franklin Watts is a division of Hachette Children's
Books, an Hachette Livre Company.
www.hachettelivre.co.uk

Photo acknowledgements: Alamy: p. 30 (Fabienne Fossez);
Corbis: pp. 20 (Anders Overgaard), 34 (Raheb Hamavandi/
Reuters); Discovery Picture Library: p. 17 (Chris Fairclough);
Getty Images: pp. 9 (Hulton Archive), 12 (Joe McNally), 15
(3D4Medical.com), 19 (Doctor Stock), 31 (Koshtra Tolle),
33 (China Photos), 36 (Bryn Lennon); istockphoto.com: cover
bottom right (Karin Lau), pp. 14 (Thomas Pullicino), 16 (Gene
Chutka), 25 (Rich Legg), 26 (Lisa Fletcher); John Birdsall Photo
Library/www.johnbirdsall.co.uk: cover top, pp. 23, 24, 28, 29,
35, 37; London Vision Clinic/Professor Dan Z. Reinstein:
p. 18; Photofusion: cover bottom left; Science Photo Library:
p. 8 (Cordelia Molloy); Shutterstock: pp. 11 (Ruben Enger),
32; Sound Foresight Ltd: p. 39; University of Southern
California/National Science Foundation.

Source credits: We would like to thank the following for
their contribution: the library of the RNIB in London for its
help with references and literature and Sarah Shulman for
her story. Mike's story originally appeared in "From a different
viewpoint" by Sally French and John Swain, published by
Jessica Kingsley Publishers.

*Please note the case studies in this book are either true life
stories or based on true life stories.*

*The pictures in the book feature a mixture of adults
and children who are and are not blind. Some of the
photographs feature models, and it should not be implied
that they are blind.*

Contents

What is blindness?

Blindness can be a disorder of the eyes, a disorder of the visual centres of the brain, or both. It results in a person's sense of vision being poor or almost absent. Sight loss is one of the most common disabilities in the UK and USA. Worldwide, blindness affects tens of millions of people.

A person who has good vision can see objects up close or far away equally clearly. However, many people have imperfect vision. They may be unable to read a book, watch television or recognise a face at a distance without the aid of glasses or contact lenses. Some of these people had good vision as a child, but needed help with near or distant vision, or both, as they grew older.

Degrees of blindess

Other people cannot see even with the help of glasses or contact lenses: they have a sight problem. These people are assessed to see whether they are sight impaired (partially sighted) or severely sight impaired (blind).

To be considered blind, a person will able to see the top letter on an eye chart only at a distance of less than three metres,

◄ *This is how a person with a visual impairment might see a street market scene – the central part of the image is a blind spot (see page 13).*

or they may be able to see the top letter at a distance of less than six metres, but with a reduced field of vision (see page 16). A blind person may also be able to see the top letter on an eye chart, but with a very narrow field of vision.

A person who is partially sighted is able to see the top letter on an eye chart at a distance of between three and six metres, or is able to read the third line down on the chart with a more narrow field of vision. A partially sighted person may be able to read the fourth line down on the chart, but with a very narrow field of vision.

A world problem

It is estimated that there are 50 million blind people in the world and perhaps 250 million who are partially sighted. Blindness is most common among the elderly and in countries where people suffer from a poor diet. The tropical diseases trachoma and onchoceriasis (see page 13) can also cause blindness.

A lack of vitamins and minerals can lead to such eye disorders as xerophthalmia, night blindness, age-related cataracts and macular degeneration (see page 13). In Britain there are about two million people with sight problems and of these, 370,000 are officially blind or partially sighted. In the USA, there are 10 million people with sight problems and 1.3 million who are registered blind or partially sighted.

▶ *Roger Bacon is often credited as the first person to develop and use a magnifying glass, the basic element of spectacles and contact lenses.*

THE FIRST SPECTACLES

The English scientist Roger Bacon (1214-92) was the first person to experiment with glass lenses to correct faulty vision. Spectacles, or eyeglasses, that use such lenses were first recorded in Italy around 1290.

Causes and effects

Some people are born blind or become blind early in childhood. Their eyes, the visual parts of their brain, or the links between the two, do not develop properly. Other people become blind through illness, an accident or old age.

The human eye is like a camera. Light enters the front of the eye. Light is focused by the cornea, a clear outer covering, and by the lens of each eye. A ring of muscle, the iris, controls the amount of light entering each eye by making an opening – the pupil – bigger or smaller. When light enters the eye, it is focused on to a sensitive layer of nerve cells, called the retina, at the back of the eye. Cells in the retina send signals to the visual centres of the brain, where they are interpreted as images or pictures. All this happens automatically and constantly when your eyelids are open. Any or all of these parts of the eye can fail to grow properly or become diseased or damaged, causing partial or total loss of sight.

Not all black and white

People who are blind do not necessarily live in complete darkness – in fact only three per cent of blind people can see nothing at all. Most blind people can tell if it is daylight or whether a light is switched on in a room. They can probably see movement, too, but cannot see any details of the shape or colour of objects. Most images they can see look fuzzy, blurred, misty or patchy. Their vision may also be limited in range: they may only be able to see clearly that which is directly in front of them or to the side. People who are partially sighted can often see enough to recognise family and friends if they are standing close by.

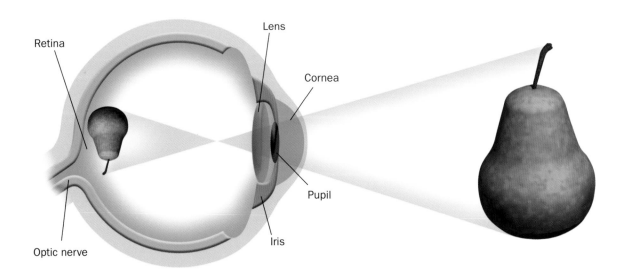

Retina

Lens

Cornea

Pupil

Iris

Optic nerve

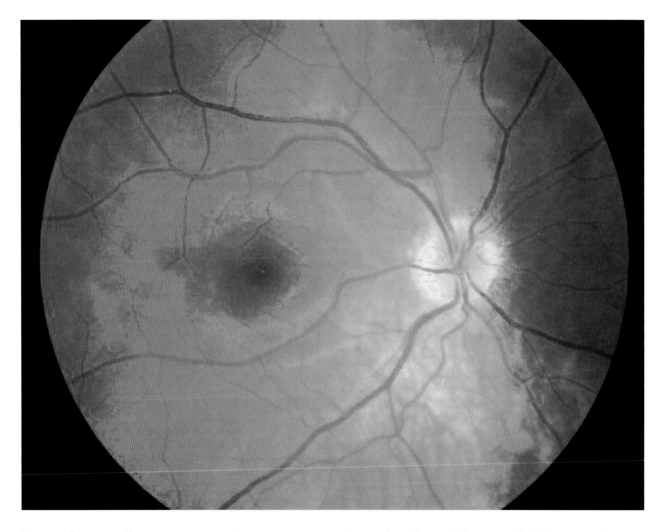

Depending on other senses

Sight is one of our most important senses, along with smell, taste, hearing and touch. Sometimes it is said that people who cannot see have sharpened their other senses, for example they are said to have a stronger sense of smell or heightened hearing. This is probably not true. However, many blind people have learned to use their other senses as much as possible to compensate for their loss of sight.

▲ *An enlarged view of the retina of the human eye shows a mass of nerve cells and a network of blood vessels that supply them with nutrients. The bright area in this image is the root of the optic nerve that links the eye to the visual centre of the brain.*

Visual impairment

Blindness and partial sight are known as visual impairment. There are many disorders and diseases that can cause it. Some of these are avoidable and curable, but others are not.

Most visual problems can be overcome if they are treated quickly. Some kinds of damage to the eyes caused by injury can be repaired. If they are not, partial sight loss can lead to blindness.

In developed countries such as those of Western Europe and North America, most visual impairment starts as people age – adults gradually lose their sight as the cells in the body no longer grow and repair themselves. Ninety-five per cent of people with sight problems are aged 65 and over. In developing countries, most blindness occurs because of poor diet and diseases caused by lack of hygiene and polluted water supplies.

▼ *In many parts of Africa there are poor standards of health and hygiene. Untreated eye infections attract insects that carry diseases. These diseases can lead to blindness.*

Disorders

Here is some information about several common disorders that can cause visual impairment:

Cataracts clouding of the lenses makes images cloudy and blurry, and colours no longer seem bright and clearly distinguishable.

Diabetes abnormalities in the retina's blood capillaries affect seeing images clearly.

Glaucoma the pressure of fluids within the eye increases, causing damage to the optic nerve that joins the retina to the brain.

Macular degeneration the macula is the central area of the retina. The cells in this area can stop working, leading to the central area of images being unclear or non-existent (see image on page 8).

Nystagmus uncontrolled movement of the eyes so that all aspects of vision are greatly reduced.

Onchoceriasis a tropical disease caused by a tiny worm that burrows through the skin. Larvae of the worm can migrate in the bloodstream to the eyes, causing partial or total blindness. It can be treated effectively with drugs.

Retinal detachment the retina becomes detached from the back of the eyeball, so vision becomes blurred and dim.

Retinitis pigmentosa cells within the retina do not function well, so that the person affected can no longer see fine detail and colour, and the area of vision may be restricted.

Trachoma a highly infectious tropical disease of the eyelids that can lead to blindness. The eyelids

become swollen and inflamed, the conjunctiva becomes rough and scarred, and the cornea becomes scratched. It can be treated with antibiotics.

Xerophthalmia the cornea and conjunctiva become dry, thickened and wrinkled because of a lack of vitamin A in the diet.

CASE NOTES

ABASI'S STORY

'My name is Abasi. I am a boy of 12 living in a village in Tanzania in East Africa. When I was a baby and young child I had good vision. I did not need to wear glasses to see well and I never had any eye infections. But I have been blind for the last four years.

In my country many children are blind as a result of trachoma, a bacterial infection of the eyelids. The bacteria are spread by flies or by contact with infected objects or with a person who has the disease.

To this day I am not sure how I caught the disease. It was probably from flies. The infection made my eyes feel itchy. I rubbed them and this made them swollen and inflamed. Gradually, over many months, my corneas became rough and scarred. Then my eyelids started to turn in, making the problem worse. Now I cannot see clearly. Soon, an international medical organisation is coming to my village to operate on my eyes, to turn the eyelids back out, and to show me how to keep my eyes clean so the problem does not get worse. But I will remain blind. I will have to learn to cope.'

Colour blindness and night blindness

The light-sensitive cells of the retina are of two types – rods and cones. Rods are sensitive to low levels of light, cones to coloured light. Sometimes the cones do not work properly, and this results in colour blindness. If the rods do not work properly, this can result in night blindness and a narrowing of one's field of vision.

Seeing colours

'Colour blindness' is not really a visual impairment, since a person with the disorder can often see well. It is better known as colour confusion, as he or she cannot distinguish colours properly. There are three types of cones which are sensitive to red, green or blue light. These colours are known as the primary colours of visible light, as our brains interpret all other colours as mixtures of these three. A person with colour confusion may lack, one, two or all three types of cones. The most common confusion is between red and green. The disorder is hereditary, meaning it runs in families, and is caused by defective genes. Genes are the chemical instructions that control how your body looks and works. The genes that affect the cones of the eye are generally passed from a mother to her sons. As a result, colour confusion occurs in about one in every 25 males, but only one in every 200 females.

Night blindness

This disorder is mostly hereditary too, but there are other causes as well, such as poor diet. The hereditary form is called retinitis pigmentosa. Retinitis pigmentosa usually develops between the ages of 10 and 30.

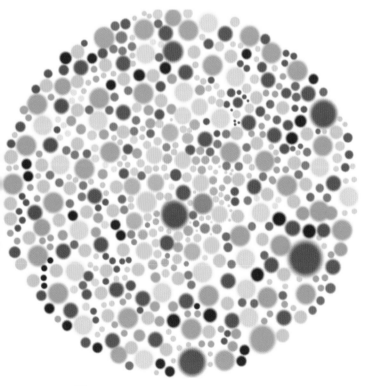

◀ *Can you see a letter or number within this circle? If you can, it means you are not colour blind. This pattern of coloured dots is used to detect 'colour confusion'.*

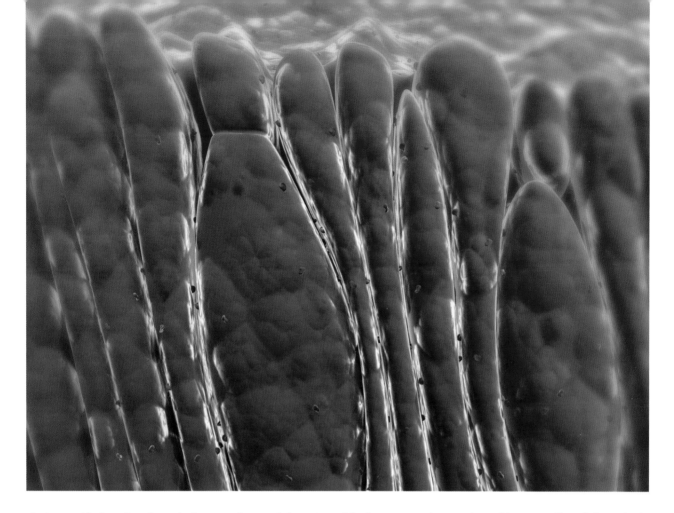

▲ *A magnified section through the central area of the retina of the human eye shows column-like cone cells tightly packed together. Cone cells contain pigments that are sensitive to various coloured rays of light.*

If your vision is normal, you will notice that in darkness your eyes get used to the low level of light. A light source such as a candle or distant street lamp will, over a few seconds or minutes, gradually look brighter. For a person with night blindness, they may not see the light source at all, and it certainly will not appear to get brighter. As rods are mostly at the sides of the retina, this person will also have poor peripheral, or side-angle, vision. People with night blindness will not see well to either side of their head, even during the day, so their field of view is limited.

Night blindness can be caused by a lack of vitamin A in the diet, as this is needed to make rhodopsin, the chemical in rods that is sensitive to light. Red meat, fish oils, green vegetables and carrots are all rich in vitamin A. Treatment involves taking vitamin A supplements, but this only stops the problem from getting worse, it does not cure it.

Vitamin A

Vitamin A is needed for the health of a variety of cells in the body. In addition to helping rods, vitamin A is also needed to keep cells of the cornea and conjunctiva of the eye healthy. People who catch measles, which causes a widespread skin rash, sometimes also get an infection which can produce similar symptoms in the eyes to xerophthalmia (see page 13). This is because vitamin A is also needed to restore healthy skin cells. A person with measles is often sensitive to bright light and should rest in a darkened room until the infection has gone away.

Eye tests

Adults aged between 16 and 60 should have their eyes tested every two years. Children should have their eyes tested every year. This helps to prevent, stop or cure any sight problems.

An eye test examines two main aspects of vision: visual acuity and peripheral vision.

Visual acuity

Visual acuity describes how good your detailed vision is (see pages 8-9). This is measured by checking how well you can read letters, numbers and symbols of decreasing size on a standard chart from a distance of six metres. A person with perfect vision can read almost the smallest letters on the chart. This person is said to have 6:6 (20:20 in feet) vision. A partially sighted person may have only 6:60 vision, meaning that at six metres from the chart, he or she can only see the very big letters. A person with perfect eyesight can see these letters from 60 metres away.

Peripheral vision

This concerns how well a person can see outside the area directly in front of their eyes. The total area of vision is called the visual field. A person with perfect vision can see clearly within a field of about 160 degrees – almost half a circle. A person

▼ *Opticians use eye charts to judge a person's visual acuity.*

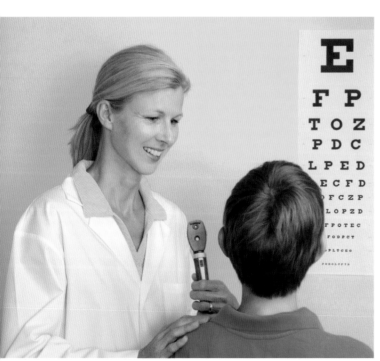

OPTICS

The study of light and vision is known as optics. An optician is someone who supplies and fits spectacles or contact lenses. An optometrist is specially trained to examine the eyes and to prescribe spectacles or contact lenses. An ophthalmologist is a doctor specialising in the diagnosis and treatment of eye disorders and diseases.

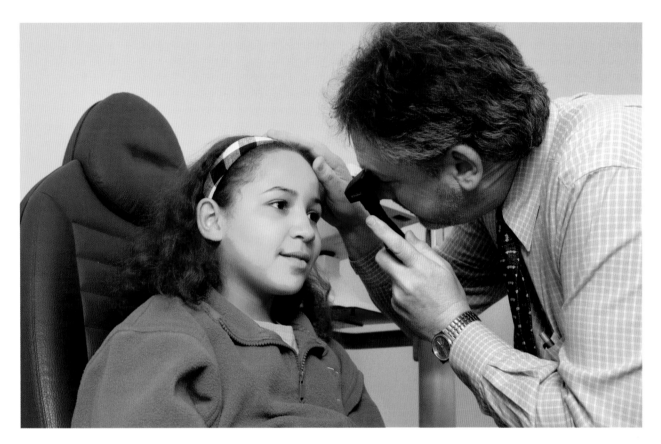

▲ *An optician uses an ophthalmoscope to examine the inside of the eye. This instrument shines a light into the eye and examines the blood vessels of the retina.*

with poor peripheral vision may see within an area of only 100 degrees: only their central vision is good. This disability is sometimes called tunnel vision. It can be caused by diabetes, a stroke or retinitis pigmentosa, when the rods of the eyes do not work properly.

Other tests

An opthalmologist or optometrist will also check for colour blindness using special colour charts that test how well a person can distinguish colours (see page 14). He or she will also examine the

cornea, lens and retina of each eye. Spectacles or contact lenses will be prescribed to improve near and/or distant vision and other defects of normal vision. For some visual impairments, specialist viewing instruments and machines may be used and surgery may be recommended.

For young children who cannot read, or people with severe eye problems or learning difficulties, tests will include measuring electrical signals in the eyes, brain and in the nerves between them. To do this, small electrical contacts are attached to the eyelids or the surface of the skull. Any disorder is highlighted by comparing a patient's electrical signals with those of a person with normal vision.

explaining... BLINDNESS

Treatments and cures

Eye problems caused by poor diet or infections can sometimes be treated with vitamin supplements and medicines. Others, including cataracts and detached retinas, can be repaired using surgery. Blindness caused by hereditary disorders cannot be corrected at all.

A few eye disorders require surgery. Cataract surgery, for example, is one of the most commonly performed surgical procedures in the world. Injuries to the eye and blood clots can be repaired or removed by surgery.

Laser treatment

In recent years, increasing numbers and types of eye disorders have been treated using laser surgery. A laser beam is a thin line or beam of light. It is very powerful and can be directed with fine precision. A laser beam can cut flesh, seal burst blood capillaries in the retina, and help to repair tears in tissues. Laser surgery is usually quick and painless.

▼ *Eye operations using laser surgery can be done without a general anaesthetic, so the patient is awake during the operation.*

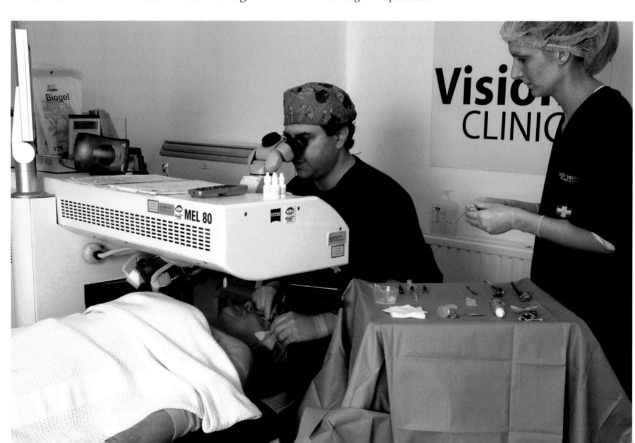

SARAH'S STORY

'My name is Sarah and I am 88 years old. About 10 years ago I developed a problem in my left eye. I was seeing bright flashes of light and showers of dark spots, or 'floaters'. I went to my local doctor. He immediately suspected a detached retina and sent me straight to an eye clinic. His diagnosis was quickly confirmed. The problem was repaired with laser treatment the next day.

After that, my vision got gradually worse. Vision in my right eye became cloudy and blurred. My optician diagnosed a cataract. A few weeks later, I had a small operation to remove the cloudy lens. The surgeon took out the lens and replaced it with a clear plastic lens. The operation was quick, simple and, although unpleasant, it was not painful. After a few weeks, the sight in that eye was almost back to normal. Everything seemed clearer and colours were certainly brighter. Next month I am due to have the cataract in my left eye operated on.'

Corneal grafting

The cornea, the transparent layer over the front of each eye, can become infected and, if not treated properly, needs replacing. This involves a small transplant operation. Healthy corneas are taken from a donor, and sewn in place of the damaged ones. The operation is done under anaesthetic and takes about an hour. As with all transplant operations, it is important that the donor and the person receiving the corneas be genetically similar, if not identical. If not, the transplanted cornea will be rejected by the body as 'foreign' tissue and another healthy cornea will have to be found.

Medicines

Medicines are used to treat infections of the eyelids, tear glands and outer surfaces of the eyeballs. They are usually applied directly to the eyes in creams, ointments and drops. To treat infections inside the eyes, antibiotics are introduced into the blood system so they are carried to capillaries in the retina and surrounding tissues. The antibiotics are given as pills, tablets or sometimes as injections.

▼ *Eye drops are an easy way of applying medicines to the outer eye.*

Coping with blindness

People who are born blind will learn how to use their other senses to manage in everyday life as they grow up. When people lose their vision later in life, they have to relearn many skills.

Blindness from birth

It is often very difficult to determine blindness at birth. However, even though very young children are unable to speak or to explain what they can or cannot see, it is still possible to assess their vision.

Professional help

As soon as a child is diagnosed as partially sighted or blind, his or her parents or guardians can get a great deal of help and support from the medical profession. The child can be examined and given

FAMOUS BLIND PEOPLE

Many people with a visual impairment have become successful. Among famous people who were born blind are Puerto Rican musician Jose Feliciano and British politician David Blunkett MP. Those who became blind include artists Edgar Degas and Claude Monet, musicians Stevie Wonder and Ray Charles, singer Andrea Bocelli, authors Helen Keller, Sue Townsend and John Milton, composers Johann Sebastian Bach and Frederick Delius, scientist Galileo Galilei and professional golfer Zohar Sharon.

spectacles to help with vision or, if appropriate, have an operation. He or she can be helped by different professionals, including a mobility officer, who is a person specially trained to help partially sighted people find their way around. A variety of optical aids, such as talking computers and magnifiers, can be provided. Reading and measuring equipment are provided with letters, numbers and symbols that are raised so they can be felt rather than viewed. Families and schools can also be provided with special tools and gadgets, such as telephones, radios and MP3 players that blind people can use on their own safely and efficiently.

Rehabilitation

Learning to cope with the onset of blindness is known as rehabilitation. Tasks that once were simple and straightforward have to be relearned and done in different ways. These include getting washed and dressed, going to school, going shopping and playing sport.

Support

People of all ages who are or become blind can feel sad and depressed. Their parents, other relations and friends have to work hard to appreciate the problems blind people experience so that they can help and support them. Blind people should be encouraged to find all the help they can get from local government bodies, schools and charitable organisations. With the right support, visually impaired people can go to ordinary schools, and do almost any job they wish.

◀ *The singer Andrea Bocelli became blind at the age of 12 due to a combination of glaucoma and an accident while playing football.*

CASE NOTES

RACHEL'S STORY

'My name is Rachel. I have been almost completely blind since birth. I like reading, playing on my computer and playing my guitar. I live at home with my parents and brother, David.

I am woken every morning by my talking alarm clock. I go straight to the bathroom to take a shower. Then I go downstairs for breakfast. I can manage on my own as my parents have put cutlery, crockery, toaster, cereals, milk, juices and spreads in set places that are easy for me to reach. Then I go upstairs to brush my teeth and get dressed. I can't see shapes very well but I can see colours. My mother lays out my clothes so I can recognise them by colour, the shapes of special buttons she has sewn on, and feeling the texture.

When David and I are ready for school, he helps me to the school bus and we make the journey together. At school, I mess around with my friends before lessons, then one of them guides me to class. In class, I do lessons like everyone else. I use a talking computer and machine that prints out my work in Braille, an alphabet of raised dots that I feel with my fingertips (see page 32). Mrs Roberts, a parent helper, puts my Braille into ordinary writing for the teacher to mark. Mrs Roberts also helps me in practical science lessons and in art.'

Optical aids

Organisations that provide help and support for blind and partially sighted people have developed more than 750 everyday items that make life easier. Many of these items are optical aids to help people make the most of the sight they have.

Reading with sight impairment

Many partially sighted people can read ordinary printed information if it is clear, large enough, well designed and well lit. People with glaucoma, for example, can see well if objects are placed close and in front of their eyes. Those with macular degeneration, a common eye condition in older people, have some vision to the sides of their eyes.

Reading and writing aids

Optical aids such as magnifiers can make letters larger and clearer. Special bookrests with built-in lighting allow reading materials to be set up in the best position and with ideal illumination. Computer keyboards with large print keys and letters or screens with black text on a contrasting background, such as yellow, can help people distinguish characters for typing. Typoscopes are cards with reading 'windows' that allow text to be read a line or word at a time, which many partially sighted people find helpful. Special writing frames and lined pads make handwriting easy and neat.

Many popular books for people of all ages are published as large print books. Computer software exists to enlarge text and images on the screen. Video magnifiers can be linked to a television and used to read magazines, newspapers, books and instructions. For those with little or no sight, books, signs and information can be printed in Braille (see page 32).

◄ *Many visually impaired people can easily read newspapers, magazines and books with the help of a simple magnifying glass.*

Everyday optical aids

All kinds of measuring devices, from clocks, rulers and scales to calculators, are made with big, bright lettering to help visually impaired people. Many of them are also designed to announce what they have measured, such as the weight or length of an object.

Reducing glare

People suffering from cataracts, or uveitis – typically a disorder of the iris and choroid, the middle layer of the eyeball – often find the brightness, or glare, from objects troublesome. One way of reducing glare is to wear glasses with special lenses that cut out the ultraviolet (UV) rays of sunshine that cause glare. These glasses can be worn on their own or over the top of ordinary glasses. Even for people with normal vision, wearing sunglasses that cut out UV light in bright sunshine is advisable. Too much glare can cause headaches.

COPING WITH UVEITIS

Nathan, aged 16, has uveitis and is partially sighted. 'My eyes are photosensitive so I wear wraparound sunglasses with UV filters. At school, I have a computer set up that has a black background, not a white one, which I find too bright to look at. When word processing, the letters and punctuation marks are made to appear in 20pt type, rather than the standard 10 or 12pt, and are displayed a line at a time.'

On the move

There are many things that help visually impaired people get around outdoors – for example, white canes, guide dogs and the help of sighted people. Some of the problems they face are obstacles on pavements, crossing roads and noisy traffic which makes it difficult for them to use their sense of hearing.

Hazardous obstacles include parked cars, lampposts, railings, roadworks, holes in pavements, sacks of rubbish and people cycling along pavements.

To help visually impaired people, towns and cities are increasingly using touch and sound signals on street furniture. These include:

- traffic lights and road crossings with bleepers signalling when it is safe to cross

- different pavement and floor surfaces to indicate platform and pavement edges, entrances and the way to stairs, lifts and escalators

- spoken announcements at stations, airports and on buses, trains and planes

- maps, signs and timetables that are raised, enlarged or displayed in Braille

- good lighting, distinct colours and large, clear lettering on signs and noticeboards.

▶ *At train stations, loudspeaker announcements provide information for blind people. Special paving stones, with raised areas at the edge of the platform, help blind and partially-sighted people to find their way on to the train.*

Understanding the problems

To get a sense of what a visually impaired person has to deal with when they are out and about, list every aspect of your journey to school. How far do you walk or travel on public transport? What obstacles and barriers do you encounter? Where do you get a travel ticket and how do you use it? How do you know where the bus or train is going and when you have reached your destination? How do you cross the roads? Now list at least 10 things that could have been done to make the journey easier for a person with sight problems.

Help, don't hinder

If you would like to help a blind or partially sighted person with a cane, first introduce yourself and make sure they know you are speaking to them. Ask them if they need any help. Do not assume they need assistance. Do not get hold of their arm, let them take yours instead, and do not walk away without saying you are leaving.

If the person has a guide dog, do not try to feed or pat the dog. This can distract the dog from its job.

Smart Hal

Mobile phone software has been developed specially for visually impaired people. Called Smart Hal, it speaks out information such as the number of the person who is calling, when the battery strength is low or when you have a voicemail message or a missed call. It can work on most modern mobile phones. Having a mobile phone is a great help to visually impaired people outdoors as it gives them more confidence to travel independently, knowing that assistance from relatives and friends is just a call away.

▲ *This blind man uses his cane and the help of a sighted girl to walk in a park. If you are helping someone who is blind, let them take your arm to steady and guide them.*

Guide dogs and canes

About one in 10 blind people use a white cane or guide dog to get around. To use either of these aids requires lots of training and practice. Blind children also learn to use white canes, but may sometimes rely on an adult to guide them, holding on to their hand or arm.

Using a cane

People who have partial sight often use a white cane. A short cane is used as a signal, perhaps only when crossing the road, to indicate to motorists that a person has a visual impairment. Totally blind people use a longer white cane to feel their way around and to touch against objects, such as kerbs and walls.

As visually impaired people walk along the street, they can also rely on sounds to judge their surroundings. For example, they will notice changes in the sound of their footsteps as they echo against walls, or the sound of people talking getting louder and then fainter. A red and white cane indicates that a person is deaf as well as blind.

Guide dogs

Some blind people feel more confident using a guide dog. Before they go outdoors, they fit a harness to their dog, then give it the basic command 'forward'. The owner is guided by the dog's movements.

▶ *The working life of a guide dog is about six and a half years, so a blind person may own several guide dogs in their lifetime.*

A guide dog is trained from an early age by a sighted person. When the dog is ready, it is matched with an owner whose walking speed and personality are suited to it. The owner and dog are then trained together for about a month before living together without supervision.

'I am blind and have a guide dog, Cloe. I go with Cloe to work every day, travelling on the subway and up in the lift to my office on the 33rd floor. For most of the day, Cloe sleeps by my desk on a blanket. Come rain or shine, every lunchtime we go out to a local store to get some food and for Cloe to go to the park. We leave my office before rush-hour to avoid any problems getting home.'
Jennifer, aged 32

GUIDE DOG HISTORY

The first known example of the special relationship between a dog and a blind person is from a wall painting in the Roman town of Herculaneum from the 1st century AD. The first attempts to train dogs to help blind people get around took place in Paris, France, in the 1780s. The practice became well established in the 1920s and 1930s, when guide dog schools were set up in Britain, France, Austria, Germany, Spain, Italy, the United States, the Soviet Union and Canada. Since then, guide dog schools have spread to almost 100 countries in the world.

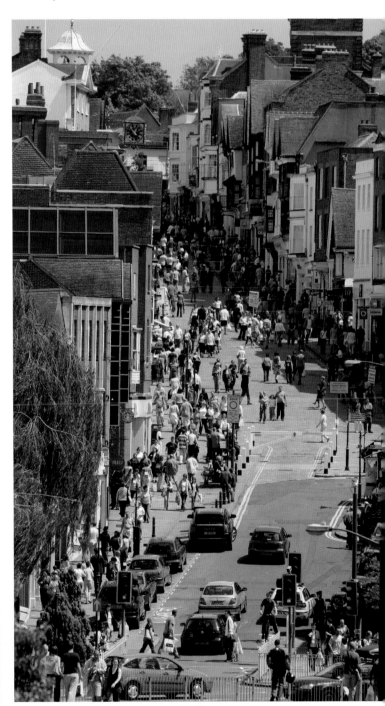

▼ *Look at all the obstacles in this busy street scene. It would be difficult for visually impaired people to find their way around.*

Home life

For many blind people, home is the easiest place to be comfortable in. They can set up furniture, gadgets and lighting just as they want, and keep them in fixed places so they do not have to search for them each time they need to use them.

Like all people with disabilities, blind peoples' lives are made easier if the people around them understand what it is like to be partially sighted or blind. If you close your eyes or wear a blindfold for a while and walk around your home, you will experience only some of the difficulties. So if you are visiting a blind person's house, consider why things are set out differently or in a set pattern or arrangement.

For those people who once had normal vision and now have poor or reduced vision due to an infection, accident or age-related disorder, think about how aspects of their vision have changed.

▼ *A resource officer from a mobile unit for the visually impaired holds up a kitchen timer with jumbo markings which are easy to see and feel. The timer emits a loud ring when the time is up.*

▲ *All kinds of electronic devices, like this home telephone, are made in versions that have large keys and visual displays with large numbers to help those with poor vision.*

The changes may include a decrease in ability to distinguish colours, to see objects close up, to see objects clearly against a similar-coloured background, to judge distances accurately, to adjust quickly to changes in lighting levels and an increase in sensitivity to light.

Here is a checklist of items that make a home user-friendly for a blind person:

• entrances, stairs and landings should be brightly and evenly lit

• sensors can make lights switch on and off automatically as the person walks by

• adjustable lamps can be used for reading, playing on the computer or playing games

• electric cables should be kept neat and tidy to avoid anyone tripping over them

• rubber pads on the corners of sharp objects help prevent injury if a person bumps into them

• walls, doors, handles and window fittings should be painted in contrasting colours so they are easy to see.

Extra help

Some people find the help they get from parents, other relatives, friends, teachers or people at work is enough. Others get lots of help from their local council, such as aids for the home, helpers to come in and do household jobs, and financial assistance.

Counselling

With sight loss, people of all ages may feel angry, afraid or sad. They may need to talk through their feelings with a skilled listener, such as a counsellor. Counsellors are usually trained to give guidance and advice. They can see people at home, school, university, work or wherever it is easiest for the blind person to get to. One area they can advise on is how to get help from your local community.

Blindness and families

Some eye disorders run in families – they are inherited or passed on from grandparents to parents and then to children. Colour confusion, for example, is inherited and affects people from birth. Other disorders are inherited, but the symptoms do not develop for some years.

Genes and inheritance

Inherited disorders are the result of receiving faulty genes during conception. Genes are the chemical messages inside cells. They are carried on strands known as chromosomes. Genes determine how a person grows and develops. They are responsible for such characteristics as sex, hair and skin colour,

▼ *A blind mother reads a story in Braille to her two young children at their home in southern Tamil Nadu, India.*

pattern of fingerprints, blood group and structure of the eyes. In reproduction, an egg from the woman is fertilised by a sperm from the man. In the process, chromosomes from the egg and sperm are combined, giving each person two copies of each gene. Depending on which of these genes are faulty, eye disorders can appear in some or all of the children born to parents with sight problems.

Inherited blindness

Some inherited forms of cataracts and defects of the cornea affect an average of 50 per cent of boys and girls in families where blindness is inherited, whereas some types of albinism (see box) do not appear for several generations and then suddenly affect just one of several children in a family. A faulty gene causing retinitis pigmentosa is often present in a female without causing any symptoms, but when this gene is passed on to her sons, the symptoms appear. The female is said to be a carrier of the disorder.

ALBINISM

Albinism is an inherited defect that affects about one in 20,000 people worldwide. A person with albinism lacks melanin, a dark colouring or pigment that gives colour to skin, hair and eyes. He or she may have white hair, pink skin and pinkish coloured eyes. Many people with albinism have problems with their vision. This is the result of an abnormal development of the retina and of problems with the nerve connections between the eye and the brain.

Risks and taking precautions

People who have close relatives with an eye disorder should get their eyes tested regularly. Inherited disorders cannot be cured and any damage they cause may not be repairable, but with early treatment good vision can be maintained. For example, chronic glaucoma can run in some families. The risk of it becoming a problem is affected by age, race and the numbers of people affected in a family. Chronic glaucoma does not usually develop before the age of 40, but it affects one in every 100 people between 40 and 65 and one in every 20 people over the age of 65. People of Afro-Caribbean origin have a greater chance of being affected by the disorder at a younger age and their symptoms are often more severe. A person with a parent, brother or sister with the disorder has a higher risk of developing the disorder than someone whose distant uncle or aunt has it.

▼ *People with albinism are sensitive to light and often have problems with their vision.*

Blindness at school

Most children who are visually impaired go to mainstream schools. They are usually provided with special books and computers to help them read and are given extra support by teaching staff and mobility teachers who help them find their way around the school.

However, some children with a visual impairment choose to attend special boarding schools specifically for blind and partially sighted children. There are advantages and disadvantages to such schools. The advantages to the children include:

- being able to learn at their own speed and in a way that is best for them

- sharing their experiences with other children who understand the disability and its problems

- having special equipment to help with everyday things they do, from learning and playing on a computer to getting washed and dressed, playing games and eating meals.

The disadvantages to the children include:

- being away from family and friends at home

- a feeling of being different from other people

- not being able to experience and share a variety of mainstream activities.

Reading, writing, arithmetic

There are two main methods of reading for visually impaired people. These are Braille and Moon.

Both involve reading by touch with the fingertips. Braille was devised in 1829 by a blind Frenchman, Louis Braille. Characters consist of patterns of dots. Braille is often written on a typewriter-like machine called a brailler, but it can be written by hand or by a computer.

▼ *Braille is a system of dots. You need a good sense of touch to feel the bumps. Braille is used in books and to make maps and diagrams.*

▲ *A partially-sighted student works on a computer during class at a school for the blind in China. In China there are 8.7 million blind people.*

Moon was devised in 1847 by a blind Englishman called William Moon. Characters take the form of raised shapes similar to those of the alphabet and numerals. They can be written on special paper using a frame and ballpoint pen.

Computers can also help with reading. Some can print Braille. Others have speech synthesisers that read out the text on a screen. All computers can be set up to display large, clear letters on a bright background.

Finger spelling

Some children are born both deaf and blind. They can learn to communicate using finger spelling – spelling out the letters of the alphabet on a person's hand with their fingers. Each letter is indicated by a particular sign or location on the palm of the hand. For example, the letter E is a touch on the top of the index finger, an O is a touch on the top of the ring finger and an H is a full hand stroke across the palm.

Blindness as an adult

In developed countries, such as those of North America and Western Europe, the main causes of visual impairment are defects of the eyes that develop with adulthood. One of the biggest challenges facing blind or partially sighted adults can be finding work.

Every day in Britain, another 100 people start to lose their sight. They have to get used to a different way of life. As adults, the main problem can be finding employment, or work. Some employers are prepared to provide equipment and training for visually impaired people – they can get help from the government to do this. Others see the disability as a problem.

Around the world

Most countries have laws to make sure visually impaired workers are treated fairly, but certain jobs, such as a bus or train driver, pilot or surgeon, are not suitable for people with limited sight. However, there are blind lawyers, politicians, musicians, computer programmers, teachers, painters, farmers, factory workers and office administrators. In Britain and the United States, about 30 per cent of visually impaired people are employed. In Spain the figure is about 75 per cent, the highest in the world, whereas in developing countries, such as Ethiopia, it is less than one per cent. In these countries, visually impaired people often have to turn to charity for financial support.

CASE NOTES

MIKE'S STORY

Mike was born visually impaired. Initially he went to a mainstream school, but he was given very little help. At age 9 he went to a boarding school for visually impaired people. He felt happy there because his needs were understood, but his education was basic.

Mike left school at 16 and worked in an office for a short time and then in a shop. He then answered a job advertisement for an audio-technician at his local university, and he remains there today. He makes recordings, teaches students and staff to make their own recordings, and builds and maintains equipment.

His biggest problem is that life is geared to people who can drive. Sometimes he cannot go out in the evenings as there is no way of getting home late. What Mike would like to see most of all is a good public transport system so that he would have as much freedom as people who can drive.

◄ *A young woman with visual impairment sits at her desk in an office using a keyboard with an audio-feedback device. In this way, she can carry out any word-processing tasks.*

Blindness, sport and leisure

Blind and partially sighted people can take part in most sports, hobbies and leisure activities. However, they may have to be adapted and played with special equipment and the help of sighted people.

Visually impaired people of all ages can play football, waterski, swim, ride a horse, run races, garden, dance, play computer and board games, and go to shows, exhibitions and art galleries. Blind people can participate in such activities in the following ways:

- play ball games by putting a bell or rattle inside the ball to help them locate it

- ride a tandem bicycle with a sighted person in front

- run a marathon alongside a sighted person who guides them

- make sculptures, pots, woven baskets and montages using their sense of touch

- act in plays and shows by rehearsing and memorising their way around the stage or with instructions called out quietly by other players

- play chess and board games with pieces that fit in holes in the gameboard

- go to the theatre and exhibitions where audio commentary is available through headphones

- fly a small aircraft following instructions from a sighted pilot.

GOING TO THE CINEMA

Louise Keel saw her first audio-described film at her local cinema in 2004. 'In the past, I needed a sighted person to come with me and describe what was happening on the screen. Thanks to the audio description I could follow the plot closely. Audio description has made a huge difference to my life.' During audio-described films, a person with impaired vision is given a headset through which they can hear a commentary describing the body language, expressions and movements of the actors and actresses.

Paralympic Games

Disabled sportspeople are able to compete internationally at the highest level in the Paralympic Games. These are held every four years, soon after the Olympic Games, and in the same cities. One of the six categories of disability for sportspeople participating in the games is visual impairment.

Famous blind sportspeople

Erik Weihenmayer is an American adventurer who, in 2001, became the first blind person to reach the summit of Mount Everest, the world's highest peak. In 2002, he completed a seven-year quest to climb the highest mountain in each of the seven continents of the world.

◄ *The winners of the Men's Visually Impaired 20-km Cross Country race at the 2006 Winter Olympics in Turin, Italy. The skier on the right acts as a guide for the skier on the left.*

▲ *A blind or partially sighted person can go horseriding with supervision and help from a sighted person. Everyone that goes horseriding should wear a protective hat or helmet to prevent any head injuries in case of a fall.*

In April 2007, Englishman Miles Hilton-Barber became the first blind person to fly from London to Sydney, Australia, in a micro-light aircraft. With the help of a co-pilot and using 'talking' flight instruments, he made the flight to raise money to help restore the sight of blind children in developing countries.

The future for blindness

Doctors and scientists are developing many different new technologies to overcome major eye problems. Some of the technologies try to improve or bypass faulty eyesight. Others are aids to mobility. Gene therapy aims to prevent inherited eye disorders occurring.

Gene therapy

In theory, faulty genes in human cells can be replaced by normal ones, or their actions 'switched off' so they no longer cause problems. In 2007, doctors in Britain carried out the world's first eye operation involving gene therapy. They tried to insert normal copies of a gene that causes Leber's amaurosis, an inherited defect of the rods and cones in the retina, into children with this problem. It will take some time to find out if the operation has been successful, but it paves the way for other inherited eye problems to be overcome using gene therapy.

Bionic eyes

Countries across the world are working hard to develop 'bionic eyes'. These could take the form of a camera worn on a cap or a pair of glasses that sends signals directly to the visual centres of the brain, where they are interpreted as images in the normal way. The signals would miss out the retina and nerves of a damaged eye.

Another optical device, the virtual retinal display, is fitted to glasses and bypasses a faulty cornea and lens to stimulate the retina. It aids, rather than replaces, normal vision. A third technique involves inserting a tiny computer chip at the back of the eye that is linked to a small video camera built into a pair of glasses. Video images are relayed to the chip, which converts them into visual signals and passes them to the brain. This will be used to overcome macular degeneration.

Both bionic eyes and virtual retinal displays are still in the developmental stage.

▼ *An artist's impression of how a bionic eye could work. A camera hidden in the glasses sends visual signals to a microchip placed in the retina.*

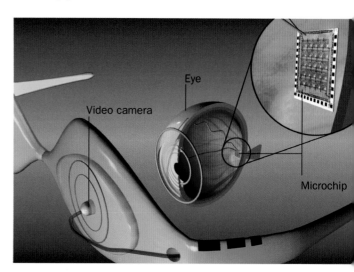

Eye

Video camera

Microchip

Eyes and teeth

Osteo-odonto-keratoprosthesis is a surgical technique being developed in the UK to restore vision in a blind person with severe damage to the cornea. It involves replacing damaged eye tissue with tissue from the person's cheek and inserting a small section made out of a human tooth and a piece of jawbone, fitted with a plastic lens. This tooth-bone-disc fragment focuses light into the eye. The tooth and bone section is taken from the patient or from a donor, fitted with the lens, then implanted in the patient's cheek to develop its own blood supply. Later, the tooth-bone-lens fragment is inserted into the eye.

Mobility aids

Just as bats and dolphins send out sounds and detect the echoes to find their way around, so scientists have created laser and radar equipment to help visually impaired people. One such device involves a headband that gives out signals which bounce off objects in front of the user. Microphones each side of the headband pick up the echoes. The blind person uses the device to support their use of a cane or guide dog. Other mobility devices include canes that send out ultrasonic or laser beams which are reflected back, causing the cane handle to send out audio signals or to vibrate. The laser beam cane indicates that there is an obstacle in the way, whereas the ultrasonic cane helps determine how far away objects are.

▶ *This type of cane emits ultrasonic waves, which bounce off objects in its path and echo back to the cane. It feeds that information to the handle, telling you how far away the object is and its position.*

Glossary

albinism a condition in which a person lacks the pigment melanin in their eyes, skin and hair

anaesthetic a combination of drugs used to avoid feeling pain

antibiotic a drug used to fight infections caused by bacteria

audio feedback a system that converts characters on a computer screen into sounds

blind a person who is blind has a high degree of vision loss. Only about three per cent of blind people are totally blind – most can distinguish between light and dark

Braille a writing system which uses a series of raised dots that can be read with the fingers

cataract a clouding of the lens of the eye

choroid layer behind the retina containing many blood capillaries

chromosomes strands of genetic material within the nucleus of each cell in the body. Chromosomes are made up of protein and DNA, or deoxyribonucleic acid, and contain many genes. Genes determine characteristics of the body

colour blindness an inherited inability to distinguish some colours, better known as colour confusion

conception the moment when a sperm fertilises an egg

cones nerve cells of the retina used for central, detailed colour vision

conjunctiva transparent skin lining the inside of the eyelids and the surface of the eyeball, except on the cornea

cornea the transparent front surface of the eye that helps to focus light onto the retina

developing countries countries where many people are poor and do not have easy access to health care

diabetes a condition in which a person has too much glucose in their blood because their body does not produce enough of the hormone insulin

eye chart a chart showing letters of various sizes that is used to assess visual acuity

finger spelling a system which uses hand shapes to spell separate letters of the alphabet

field of vision the amount people can see without moving their heads

gene the basic unit of heredity by which characteristics are passed from one generation to the next

general anaesthetic a combination of drugs that numbs the whole body and causes loss of consciousness

glaucoma a group of disorders of the eye resulting from raised pressure inside the eye

inheritance the process of passing on physical characteristics from parents to their offspring

iris a ring of muscle that forms the coloured part of the eye and has a central hole, called the pupil

laser a thin and powerful beam of light

lens the transparent disc inside the eye that focuses light onto the retina

macula the central part of the retina that contains mostly cones

magnifier a lens that makes things look bigger

Moon a writing system which uses raised letters similar to the alphabet. Moon is easier to learn than Braille for those who have become blind later in life

nerve cells/neurones cells in the body that make up the nervous system, including the brain and sense organs. They communicate with one another and other parts of the body via electrical signals

night blindness a condition in which a person has difficulty seeing in low light

nystagmus unstable or 'wobbly' eyes

ophthalmologist a doctor who deals with disorders of the eyes

optic nerve the link between the retina of the eyes and the visual centres of the brain

optician/optometrist someone who examines the eyes for defects and prescribes corrective treatment, such as glasses, when necessary

partially sighted when someone has a less severe loss of vision than a blind person. Partially sighted people can see more than blind people, but less than sighted people

peripheral the area of vision surrounding the main central area or above, below and to the sides of one's eyes

photosensitive sensitive to light

retina the layer at the back of the eye made up of rod and cone cells that are sensitive to light

rods nerve cells in the retina used for peripheral vision and seeing in low-intensity light

tunnel vision when the field of view is limited to what is directly in front of a person

visual acuity a measure of how much detail one can see

visually impaired people who are blind or partially sighted

Further information

Books

Non-Fiction

Blindness (Diseases and Disorders),
Hal Marcovitz, *Lucent Books, 2008*

Disorders of Vision in Children,
Richard Bowman, Ruth Bowman and
Gordon Dutton, *RNIB, 2001*

Living with Blindness, Patsy Westcott,
Hodder Wayland, 2002

My Friend is Blind, Nicola Edwards,
Chrysalis Children's Books, 2004

**The World At Her Fingertips: The Story of Helen
Keller (Scholastic Biography),** Joan Dash,
Scholastic, 2002

Think About Being Blind, Peter White,
Chrysalis Children's Books, 2004

**Vision Without Sight: Human Capabilities
(Shockwave),** Susan Brocker,
Scholastic Library Publishing, 2007

What Does it Mean to Be Blind?,
Louise Spilsbury, *Heinemann, 2003*

Fiction

Tangerine, Edward Bloor,
Harcourt Children's Books, 1998

The Storyteller's Beads, Jane Kurtz,
Gulliver Books, 1998

Films

The Miracle Worker
Playfilm Productions, 1962
The story of Helen Keller.

Ray
Universal Studios, 2004
The story of blind musician Ray Charles.

Websites

www.actionforblindpeople.org.uk
Action for Blind People is a UK organisation which
ensures that blind and partially sighted people
receive practical support in all aspects of their lives.
The website, which has been designed specially
to be user-friendly for the visually impaired, offers
employment advice, news and information about
schemes such as Actionnaires, which are sports
clubs for blind and partially sighted children.

www.afb.org
American Foundation for the Blind website
contains helpful information and advice for blind
and visually impaired people of all ages, as well
as news and statistics. Learn how to read the
Braille alphabet on the AFB's Braillebug webpage
www.afb.org/braillebug/braille_deciphering.asp

www.britishblindsport.org.uk
The British Blind Sport website provides information
on the many sports activities it runs for blind and
visually impaired people in the UK and abroad.

www.gdba.org.uk

The Guide Dogs for the Blind Association website offers lots of information about how guide dogs are trained, the association's campaigns and fundraising events, as well as the opportunity to sponsor a puppy.

www.nbcs.org.uk

The NBCS aims to help children and young people with visual impairment achieve their goals in the fields of education and sports. The NBCS offers advice, large print books, equipment and even recreational programmes.

www.rnib.org.uk

Royal National Institute of Blind People (RNIB) is a UK charity offering support, information and advice. The charity campaigns to eliminate avoidable sight loss and supports research into the causes and latest treatments of eye disease.

www.visionaustralia.org.au

The website of Vision Australia, an association that describes itself as a 'living partnership between people who are blind, sighted or have low vision'. The association provides services to children, such as handmade story-telling kits containing brailled and audio storybooks along with toys and objects. Read about seeing eye dogs in Australia.

Note to parents and teachers: Every effort has been made by the Publishers to ensure that these websites are suitable for children, that they are of the highest educational value, and that they contain no inappropriate or offensive material. However, because of the nature of the Internet, it is impossible to guarantee that the contents of these sites will not be altered. We strongly advise that Internet access is supervised by a responsible adult.

Index

These are the list of contents for each title
in Explaining:

Asthma
What is asthma? • History of asthma • Increase in asthma • Who has asthma? • Healthy lungs • How asthma affects the lungs • What triggers asthma? • Asthma and allergies • Diagnosing asthma • Preventing an attack • Relieving an attack • What to do during an attack • Growing up with asthma • Living with asthma • Asthma and exercise • Future

Autism
What is autism? • Autism: a brief history • The rise of autism • The autistic spectrum • The signs of autism • Autism and inheritance • The triggers of autism • Autism and the body • Autism and mental health • Can autism be treated? • Living with autism • Autism and families • Autism and school • Asperger syndrome • Autism and adulthood • The future for autism

Blindness
What is blindness? • Causes and effects • Visual impairment • Colour blindness and night blindness • Eye tests • Treatments and cures • Coping with blindness • Optical aids • Guide dogs and canes • Home life • On the move • Blindness and families • Blindness at school • Blindness as an adult • Blindness, sport and leisure • The future for blindness

Cerebral Palsy
What is cerebral palsy? • The causes of cerebral palsy • Diagnosis • Types of cerebral palsy • Other effects of cerebral palsy • Managing cerebral palsy • Other support • Technological support • Communication • How it feels • Everyday life • Being at school • Cerebral palsy and the family • Into adulthood • Raising awareness • The future

Cystic Fibrosis
What is cystic fibrosis? • A brief history • What causes cystic fibrosis? • Screening and diagnosis • The effects of cystic fibrosis • How is cystic fibrosis managed? • Infections and illness • A special diet • Clearing the airways • Physical exercise • Cystic fibrosis and families • Cystic fibrosis at school • Living with cystic fibrosis • Living longer • New treatments • Gene therapy

Deafness
What is deafness? • Ears and sounds • Types of deafness • Causes of deafness • Signs of deafness • Diagnosis • Treating deafness • Lip reading • Sign language • Deafness and education • Schools for the deaf • Deafness and adulthood • Technology • Deafness and the family • Fighting discrimination • Latest research

Diabetes
What is diabetes? • Type 1 diabetes • Type 2 diabetes • Symptoms and diagnosis • Medication • Hypoglycaemia • Eyes, skin and feet • Other health issues • Healthy eating and drinking • Physical activity • Living with diabetes • Diabetes and families • Diabetes at school • Growing up with diabetes • The future for diabetics

Down's syndrome
What is Down's syndrome? • Changing attitudes • Who has Down's Syndrome? • What are chromosomes? • The extra chromosome • Individual differences • Health problems • Testing for Down's Syndrome • Diagnosing at birth • Babies • Toddlers • At school • Friendships and fun • Effects on the family • Living independently • Down's syndrome community

Epilepsy
What is epilepsy? • Causes and effects • Who has epilepsy? • Partial seizures • Generalised seizures • Triggers • Diagnosis • How you can help • Controlling epilepsy • Taking medicines • Living with epilepsy • Epilepsy and families • Epilepsy at school • Sport and leisure • Growing up with epilepsy • The future for epilepsy

Food allergy
What are food allergies? • Food allergies: a brief history • Food aversion, intolerance or allergy? • What is an allergic reaction? • Food allergies: common culprits • Anaphylaxis • Testing for food allergies • Avoiding allergic reactions • Treating allergic reactions • Food allergies on the rise • Food allergies and families • Food allergies and age • Living with food allergies • 21st century problems • The future for food allergies